# THE TALE OF THE DAYS
# THE KING HAS MADE

# LUISETTE KRAAL

Copyright ©
Drs. Luisette Kraal
www.Luisettekraal.com
Publisher: Saved to Serve International Ministries
Book illustrator: R. Shankar

Title chosen by students of Timothy Christian Schools.
The winning group was: 1. Nathan Gehrke
2. Aviel Cornett
3. Faith Brown
4. Anna White

Manufactured in the USA 2022
ISBN: 978-1-7379647-2-8

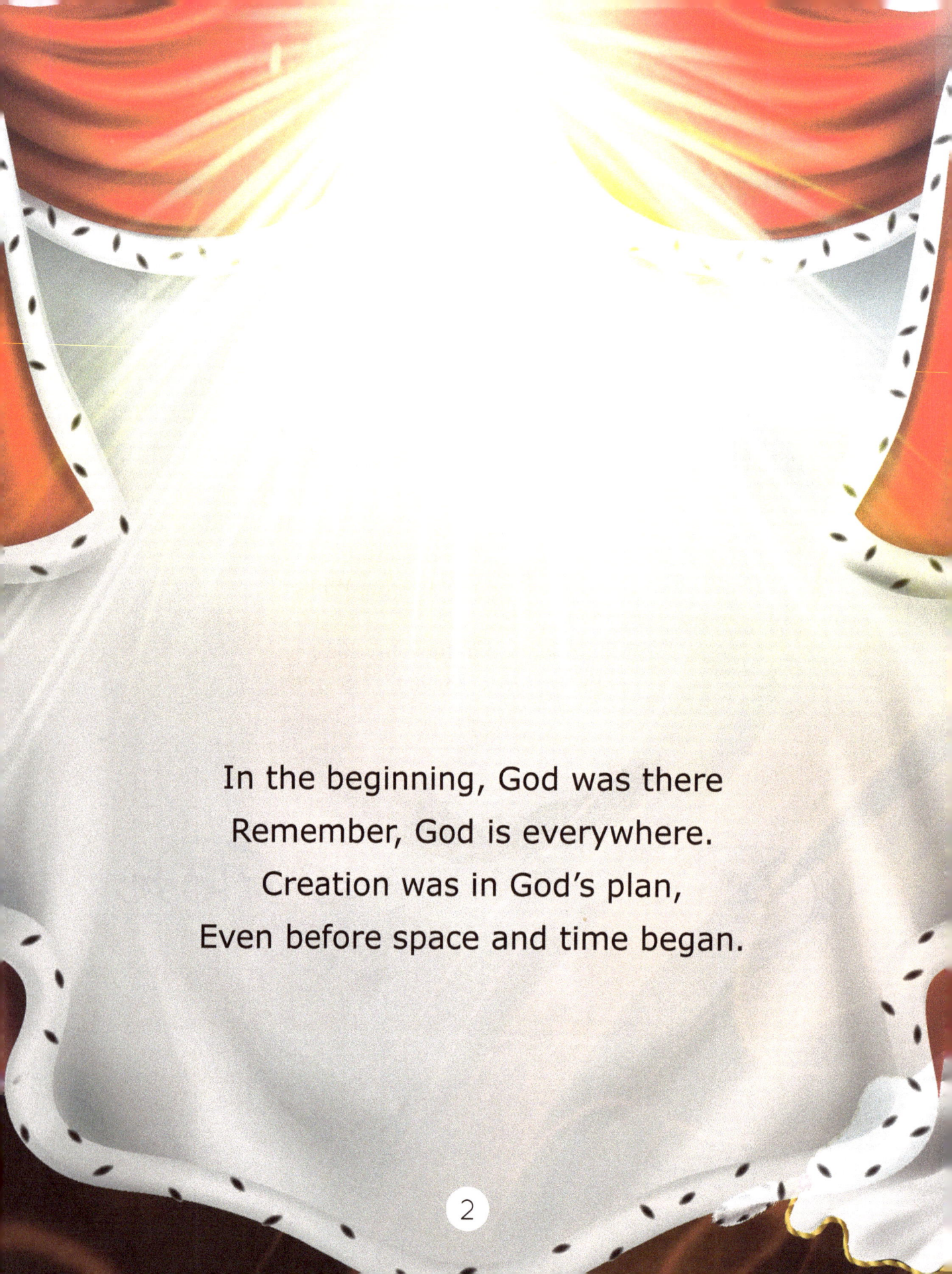

In the beginning, God was there
Remember, God is everywhere.
Creation was in God's plan,
Even before space and time began.

# DAY 1

Genesis 1:4 And God saw that the light was good.

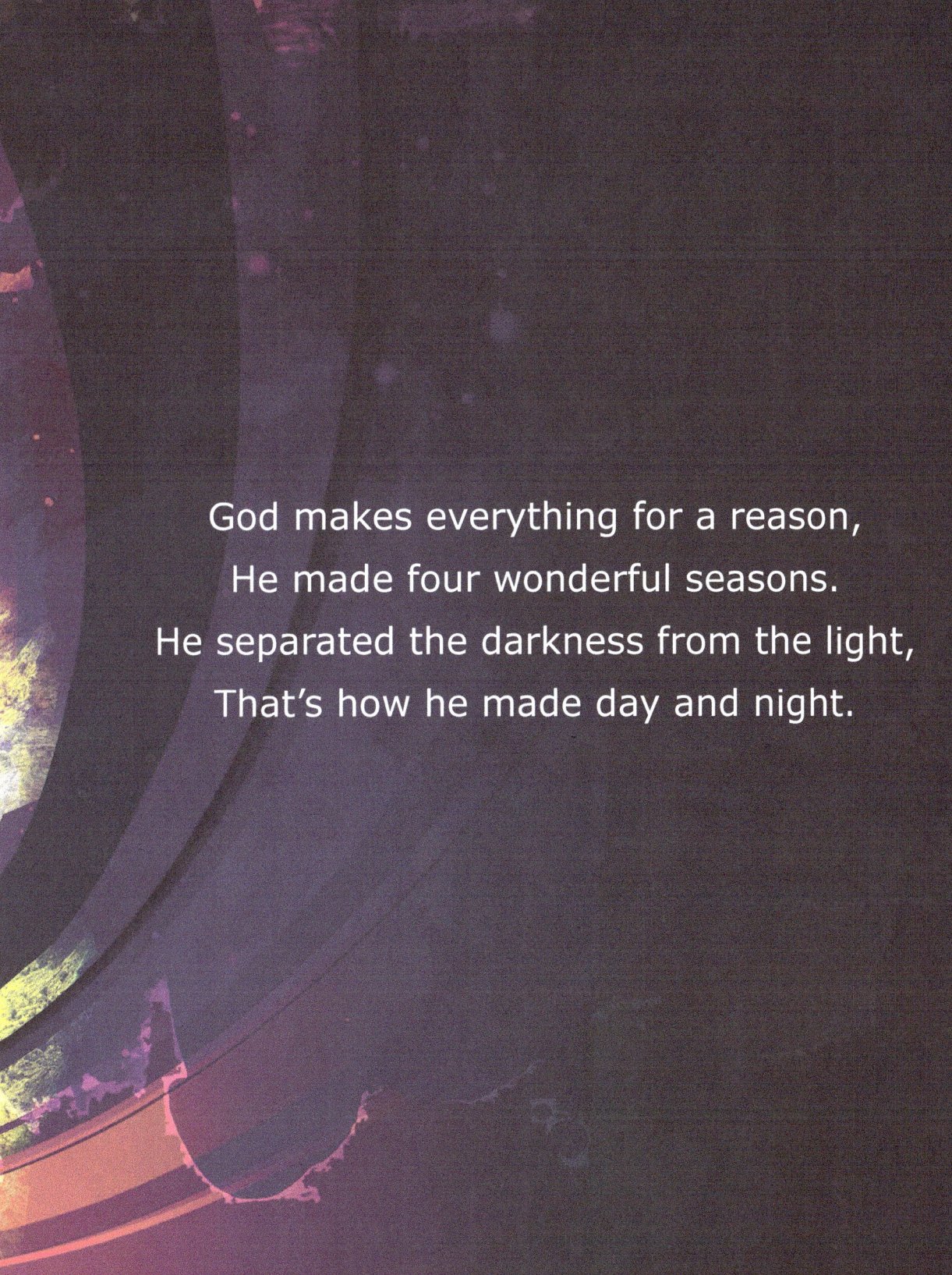

God makes everything for a reason,
He made four wonderful seasons.
He separated the darkness from the light,
That's how he made day and night.

# DAY 2

Genesis 1:10 And God saw that it was good.

God used his words to speak,
And that is how he made the week.
God speaks and things come into being,
The whole wide world that we're now seeing.

A spectacular dome was created;
The waters were then separated.
The water was above and below;
God called the dome sky,
and it was so.

Genesis 1:12 And God saw that it was good.

Now God gathered the water in one place.
What will he do with the other space?
He made land called earth to appear;
Everything was made with such love and care.

The same God named the water sea
Where we can swim and play for free.

The earth looked rich but oh-so brown
Until the plants grew in the ground.

For the night, the moon did rule;
This was so incredibly cool.
For the day, he made the sun;

In the light, we play and run.
He also made the twinkling stars,
Even Saturn, Jupiter, and Mars.

On the next day, God did create
The birds and sea creatures, each with their mate.
In every size, from big to small,
From tiny to large, he blessed them all.
God told them all to multiply,
He wanted them to live and not to die.

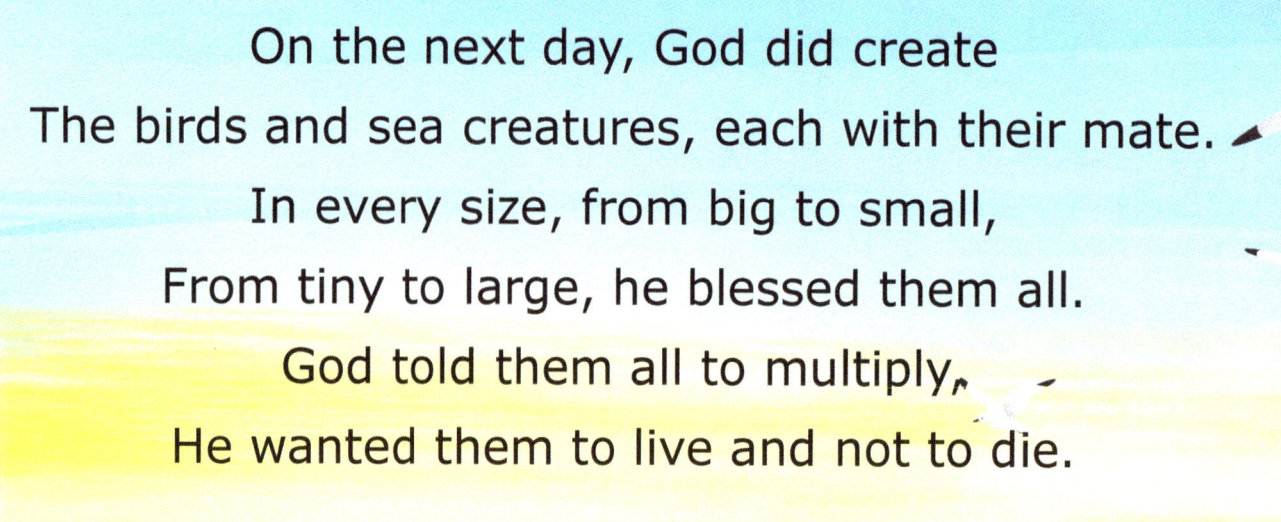

# DAY 6

Genesis 1:25 And God saw that it was good.

He created animals both wild and tame.
The great big earth was never the same.
He made the lions, tigers, dogs, and cats,
As well as bears and hamsters and rats.

The Father, Son, and Holy Spirit gave a nod
To man and woman in the image of God.
He told them to eat the fruits and seeds,
And for the animals, he gave plants and leaves.

# DAY 7

Genesis 1:31 And God saw everything that he had made, and behold, it was very good.

On day seven, all was blessed.
And God took a breath and a nice long rest.
He completed his work, his beautiful creation,
And he was filled with such elation.

**The Creation of the World**

**1** In the beginning, God created the heavens and the earth. **2** The earth was without form and void, and darkness was over the face of the deep. And the Spirit of God was hovering over the face of the waters.

**3** And God said, "Let there be light," and there was light. **4** And God saw that the light was good. And God separated the light from the darkness. **5** God called the light Day, and the darkness he called Night. And there was evening and there was morning, the first day.

**6** And God said, "Let there be an expanse[a] in the midst of the waters, and let it separate the waters from the waters." **7** And God made[b] the expanse and separated the waters that were under the expanse from the waters that were above the expanse. And it was so. **8** And God called the expanse Heaven.[c] And there was evening and there was morning, the second day.

**9** And God said, "Let the waters under the heavens be gathered together into one place, and let the dry land appear." And it was so. **10** God called the dry land Earth,[d] and the waters that were gathered together he called Seas. And God saw that it was good.

**11** And God said, "Let the earth sprout vegetation, plants[e] yielding seed, and fruit trees bearing fruit in which is their seed, each according to its kind, on the earth." And it was so. **12** The earth brought forth vegetation, plants yielding seed according to their own kinds, and trees bearing fruit in which is their seed, each according to its kind. And God saw that it was good. **13** And there was evening and there was morning, the third day.

**14** And God said, "Let there be lights in the expanse of the heavens to separate the day from the night. And let them be for signs and for seasons,[f] and for days and years, **15** and let them be lights in the expanse of the heavens to give light upon the earth." And it was so. **16** And God made the two great lights—the greater light to rule the day and the lesser light to rule the night—and the stars. **17** And God set them in the expanse of the heavens to give light on the earth, **18** to rule over the day and over the night, and to separate the light from the darkness. And God saw that it was good. **19** And there was evening and there was morning, the fourth day.

**20** And God said, "Let the waters swarm with swarms of living creatures, and let birds[g] fly above the earth across the expanse of the heavens." **21** So God created the great sea creatures and every living creature that moves, with which the waters swarm, according to their kinds, and every winged bird according to its kind. And God saw that it was good. **22** And God blessed them, saying, "Be fruitful and multiply and fill the waters in the seas, and let birds multiply on the earth." **23** And there was evening and there was morning, the fifth day.

<sup>24</sup> And God said, "Let the earth bring forth living creatures according to their kinds—livestock and creeping things and beasts of the earth according to their kinds." And it was so. <sup>25</sup> And God made the beasts of the earth according to their kinds and the livestock according to their kinds, and everything that creeps on the ground according to its kind. And God saw that it was good.

<sup>26</sup> Then God said, "Let us make man[h] in our image, after our likeness. And let them have dominion over the fish of the sea and over the birds of the heavens and over the livestock and over all the earth and over every creeping thing that creeps on the earth."

<sup>27</sup> So God created man in his own image,
  in the image of God he created him;
  male and female he created them.

<sup>28</sup> And God blessed them. And God said to them, "Be fruitful and multiply and fill the earth and subdue it, and have dominion over the fish of the sea and over the birds of the heavens and over every living thing that moves on the earth." <sup>29</sup> And God said, "Behold, I have given you every plant yielding seed that is on the face of all the earth, and every tree with seed in its fruit. You shall have them for food. <sup>30</sup> And to every beast of the earth and to every bird of the heavens and to everything that creeps on the earth, everything that has the breath of life, I have given every green plant for food." And it was so. <sup>31</sup> And God saw everything that he had made, and behold, it was very good. And there was evening and there was morning, the sixth day.

**The Seventh Day, God Rests**

**2** Thus the heavens and the earth were finished, and all the host of them. <sup>2</sup> And on the seventh day God finished his work that he had done, and he rested on the seventh day from all his work that he had done. <sup>3</sup> So God blessed the seventh day and made it holy, because on it God rested from all his work that he had done in creation.

Genesis 1:1-31

Genesis 2:1-2

# THE TALES FROM THE BIBLE
## by
# LUISETTE KRAAL

The Tale of the
House on the Rock

The Tale of the
The Farmer who Lost his Sheep

The Tale of the
Camel and the Eye of a Needle

Jonah in the Smelly Belly of the fish

# HOPPER
## Needs Clean Water

www.ingramcontent.com/pod-product-compliance
Lightning Source LLC
Chambersburg PA
CBHW080608170426
43209CB00007B/1374